MONSTER KNOWS

PATTERNS

BY LORI CAPOTE   ILLUSTRATE

PICTURE WINDOW BOOKS

a capstone imprint

A birthday party's starting now.
It's time to **CELEBRATE.**

Let's find some **PARTY PATTERNS.**

Birthday Monster
just can't wait!

3

Lets count the pairs
of monster guests.
Here's **2** and **4** ghoul friends.

6

8

This pattern of 2s
is easy to see.
That's **6** and **8** and
10!

Monsters wear big birthday hats—
1 STRIPED, 2 SPOTTED, and then ...

Another **STRIPED** hat in the row!

WHICH HATS COME NEXT, MY FRIEND?

Monsters frost some mud pies with **PINK** and **GREEN** and **WHITE**.

What color is on top of green?

Monster gets it RIGHT!

UP, DOWN, UP, DOWN, UP, DOWN, UP, DOWN,

on Monster's trampoline.

This one jumps until he's sick,
and then he looks so **GREEN!**

Monsters build a wall of gifts:

TALL, MEDIUM,
TALL, SMALL.

Which gift do they need next?

Is it SMALL, or is it TALL?

It's time to have some birthday fun.

Let's pin a tail on snake!

3 RED, 1 BLUE, 3 RED, 1 BLUE—
Which tail should Monster take?

They play The Grumpy Monster game.
3 MOVES—each one repeats.

FIST SHAKE

MAKE FACE

STOMP FEET

What comes after make a face?
STOMP those monster FEET!

FIST SHAKE

MAKE FACE

Piñata bursts. The prizes spill.

Monster grabs **3 WORMS.**

3 more make
6 on his lips.

9 WORMS
will surely squirm!

Each friend here grabs a crayon to make this birthday wall.

How many spiders with **LONG LEGS** should the monsters draw?

WE sang and laughed.
WE ate and yelled,
"BAD MONSTER DAY TO YOU!"

Now Monster's friends all say **GOOD-BYE**,
then leave us **TWO BY TWO**.

Internet Sites

FactHound offers a safe, fun way to find Internet sites related to this book. All of the sites on FactHound have been researched by our staff.

Here's all you do:

Visit *www.facthound.com*

Type in this code: 9781404879492

Super-cool stuff!

Check out projects, games and lots more at
www.capstonekids.com

Look for all the books in the series:

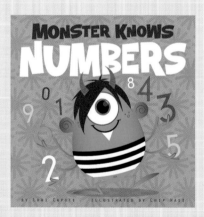

Thanks to our adviser for his expertise, research, and advice:
Terry Flaherty, PhD, Professor of English
Minnesota State University, Mankato

Editor: Shelly Lyons
Designer: Ashlee Suker
Art Director: Nathan Gassman
Production Specialist: Laura Manthe
The illustrations in this book were created digitally.

Picture Window Books are published by Capstone,
1710 Roe Crest Drive, North Mankato, Minnesota 56003
www.capstonepub.com

Library of Congress Cataloging-in-Publication Data
Capote, Lori, 1966-
Monster knows patterns / by Lori Capote ; illustrated by Chip Wass.
pages cm. — (Monster knows math)
ISBN 978-1-4048-7949-2 (library binding)
ISBN 978-1-4048-8040-5 (board book)
ISBN 978-1-4795-0184-7 (eBook PDF)
1. Pattern perception—Juvenile literature. I. Wass, Chip, 1965- illustrator. II. Title.
BF294.C365 2013
516'.15—dc23   2012029717

Artistic Effects
Shutterstock, background texture (throughout)

Printed in the United States of America in
North Mankato, Minnesota.
092012   006933CGS13